Student Ministry 101

101

Welcome To Student MInistry

Stewart Flageolle

ISBN 978-93-5667-375-5
© Stewart Flageolle 2023
Published in India 2023 by Pencil

Contributors:
Editor: Christina Flageolle

A brand of
One Point Six Technologies Pvt. Ltd.
123, Building J2, Shram Seva Premises,
Wadala Truck Terminal, Wadala (E)
Mumbai 400037, Maharashtra, INDIA
E connect@thepencilapp.com
W www.thepencilapp.com

Author biography

Stewart Flageolle is student pastor and author with a passion to see other student pastors succeed in the calling that God has placed on their lives. Stewart, and his wife Christina, have twenty years of student ministry experience and desire to see students lead a life that is pleasing to God. They live with their two children in Marionville, in southwest Missouri.

CONTENTS

Acknowledgements

I would like to thank all of those who encouraged me while writing this book. First, I want to thank God for allowing me to have gone through the seasons that are in this book. With His guidance, I truly feel that other student pastors will be able to lead this, and future, generations in a Godly way. Thank you to my wife, Christina, and my two boys, Uriah and Thaddaeus, for always encouraging me and lifting me up when I wanted to quit. Thank you to my mom and dad for raising me in a Godly home, showing me the value of living out faith. Thank you to my pastor, Kevin Inmon, for being a leader who thinks about others first, and not himself. Thank you to all of my church family and friends who have lived life with me over that last several years.

Introduction

Anger, frustration, and confusion. Chaos, and stress. Joy, love, and grace. All of these are the emotions I have felt in student ministry. Even right now as I sit here in my office writing, I find myself planning and preparing for the whirlwind of emotions that will come from student ministry. Preparing my mind, and my heart, for any of these or a mixture of them all, I know I will experience them.There is a saying that my pastor continues to repeat, "Choose Joy," What a concept! Choosing to have joy when I am angry, or choosing it in the middle of chaos, we can choose to have joy from the Lord, and know that He is our strength. As ministry leaders, we can sometimes lose focus on what really matters, because of emotions, and due to the distraction, we can start to focus on other things outside of God and His plan. No matter the emotions, no matter the months of planning, no matter where you thought you should be, God has a perfect plan for you in His ministry. As we dig through God's word together, and share life experiences, let us let go of our emotions and distraction and allow Him to move in our hearts.

"God, we thank you for this time. We thank you for the ability to call you father, and friend.

We ask, now, for you to free our minds and our hearts of emotions and distractions and choose joy.

God, we yield our time to you, and we welcome your presence.

Amen."

Welcome To Student Ministry

So You Want To Be A Student Pastor Huh? (Section 1)

I remember this one Sunday, after our student ministry meeting. The student pastor, from when I was a teenager, started asking us what we were going to do after high school. Everyone started spouting off answers, except for me. I hadn't really thought about it before. Granted, I was only a freshman in High School and didn't really know what I wanted to do, but I wanted to give him an answer. "I'm going to be a student pastor", I shouted. He smiled and said, "Cool!". I didn't realize then what the weight of that would mean throughout my high school, college and present adult life. I mean, after all, how hard could it be? How hard could it be to show up, have service, and go home?

Let me tell you from personal experience, being a student pastor isn't for the faint of heart. A student pastor isn't something that you just show up and do, it isn't a nine to five, and it isn't something that you take lightly. Pastoring students is a vital part of the well oiled machine that God has created. If we aren't careful, the students we are trying to reach will scatter into the world, without being biblically rooted. Without the foundation, you will teach them, they WILL leave the faith behind. That is why it's important to know a few things. What is a student pastor, what is a student ministry, and why student ministry is important. Maybe you are fresh out of seminary or maybe you are just somebody who is willing to fill a need. Maybe students are your secondary job as an associate pastor. No matter what brought you here, you need to know what these things are if you plan to have any kind of success for the future of that ministry. Hopefully, these next few things will help guide you through the deep waters that student ministry is, so let's begin.

What Is A Student Pastor?

So what is a student pastor? There actually isn't a definition for the term, student pastor. Why is that? The short answer is that the term student pastor is something that the modern church invented. An article by, The Youth Coalition Group, states that there weren't any youth/student related ministries on a regular basis until the 1940's. Wow! So, if we can't define a student pastor, let's define just the word pastor. If we were to look at one of the definitions of what a pastor is, we would find that a pastor is a person having spiritual care over a number of persons. So all of these different titles; youth pastor, student pastor, kids pastor, nextgen, director, student ministry pastor, and family pastor were all created by us to service a need.

Because of this, some people view a student pastor as a babysitter with a glorified title. That's obviously not true, but people actually believe that. Some people think that you are just there to watch their kids so they can have a night out, get paid, and send them home. Being a student pastor is more than just watching kids. It's this world view that is so dangerous. This world view devalues what you, as a student pastor, bring to your students each week. This is something that has been on my mind for a long time, and I can tell you that I completely disagree with this view. A student pastor can play a huge part in the lives of students. Like senior pastors, student pastors are also trusted with the spiritual development of a number of persons. So what is a student pastor? It is a pastor of students. It is a lifestyle that is immersed in the teenage realm. It's someone who will be there for students at two in the morning because of a breakup. It's someone who will preach the gospel regardless of what the current culture is. A student pastor is someone who invests and doesn't babysit. They partner with parents, not isolate them. They are a rare breed who can be there through it all and never quit. That is a student pastor. That is what we need to strive for in order to enact change. In order to do that, you have to understand your role.

What Is Your Role As A Student Pastor?

Some people often wonder what it is that you should do for your students. Oftentimes, people assume that your only role is a spiritual mentor that tells them about God on your youth night. That could NOT be farther from the truth. While you aren't their biological parent, you should be playing a huge role in students' lives. Think about it. When they have questions, you should be there to answer. When they make bad choices and their parents call you, you should be there. When they are getting ready to graduate college, and haven't been in your student ministry for four years, you should be there. Your role is to be a foundation, a rock, and a hard place. An immovable object in their lives. This is why student ministry is hard. The typical student pastor will stay at a church, no longer than, twenty four months. That's an awful statistic, but I use it to open your eyes to the truth. I truly believe that the reason for this is because student pastors do not know what their overall role is and, yes, there is a difference between a role and a job description.

The bottom line is that you are to stand in the gap. You are supposed to be there for students no matter what it is. It's not a job. It's not a means to an end. Student ministry is a lifestyle and your role is to live life with the students that God brings to you. As we move through these next sections, we will talk more about how to do that.

What Is Student Ministry?

So we've talked about what your role is in student ministry, but now we need to define what student ministry is. Student ministry is anything that you do to minister to, and reach students. Whether it is a lock-in at your church, or just creating a space for them to call their own, it can, and will, look differently for everyone. There isn't just one successful blueprint for student ministry. There are different cultures, personalities, leadership styles, and completely different worlds for each house of worship. Before you can define your student ministry you need to determine those few things. So what does your ministry look like? Are you looking at having Sunday school for teens? Maybe it's the traditional Wednesday night services. Maybe it's a small group at a leader's house. It could be a Bible study at your local fast food chain. Whatever you do, make sure that you are following God's plan and are willing to get uncomfortable. Getting uncomfortable equals growth. I know what you're thinking, " I'm just getting started. Why are we talking about growth?". Believe it or not, creating a ministry immediately encourages growth. Think about it. You went without that particular ministry to bringing one to life. The biggest issue, when creating any ministry, is figuring out what works. This goes back to the culture topic again. Whatever culture your church has, will show you what will work in reaching students.

Let me give an example. At our church, we have contemporary worship, small groups, a dream team, and a congregation that wants to be in the community as much as they possibly can. So, when we looked at the culture we wanted to have in our student ministry, we immediately implemented things from the culture of our church as a whole. We started with small groups, had worship songs that were upbeat and up to date, and we had leaders who wanted to go and do things. That was almost three years ago. So, what does it look like now? The culture had to change. Small groups turned into jr.high and high school, worship changed from youtube to live worship, and instead of only adults leading areas we created student leader roles. Keep that in mind. Change, or the right change, will bring substantial growth. I don't necessarily mean numbers, but growth will happen. So whatever is working right now, probably won't within the next couple years and you need to be willing to get out of your comfort zone to continue to see growth, spiritual and physical.

Why Is Student Ministry Important?

It doesn't feel like it sometimes, but student ministry is important. For some students, this may be the only time they get to get out of the house. For others, it's a place where they can feel safe. The reason that student ministry is important is that it gives students an opportunity to be a part of something. They get to be a part of a community of believers and it gives them a chance to use their gifts, talents and abilities that God gave them. Think about when you were a teenager. What would you have done if you wouldn't have had an outlet for your gifts, talents and abilities. I know where I was heading and it wasn't good. Luckily, I had adults who believed in me, prayed with me, and never gave up on me. You aren't just showing up on Wednesdays. You are growing the next generation of leaders and world changers. The next wave of revival starts with you being obedient to God. The smallest spiritual nudge from you could be exactly what your students need to grow to the next level. That is the ultimate importance. Being there when they need you. No matter if it's a phone call at 2am, or staying later to talk with their parents. ALL of it matters, and is very important. Student ministry should be a place where there isn't any judgment. It should only be a place that allows the spirit of God to move through each student and encourages them to do what God has called them to.

As we move into the next chapters, I want you to ask yourselves these questions.

Is student ministry important to me? Why am I serving as a student pastor?

How can I make my best better?

The Good

It was the summer of 2004, and I had just graduated from high school. I was fresh off summer youth camp and our group had just experienced a tremendous breakthrough. There was so much life change, you could smell it in the air (or maybe it was body odor from the camp activities, who knows). I was excited to be a part of that group and was ready to dive headfirst into student ministry. Then it all changed, and I was afraid.

The biggest fear I had ever experienced was happening. No more mom or dad. No more, "Sure, I can pick you up after school." It was all on me. All on the eighteen-year-old college freshmen that did not have a job, did not really know the Word, and only knew a couple of people on campus. I started to have anxiety as I walked to my first class. What was I thinking!?

I look back at it now and laugh as I sit here. Those were some good times. Hmmm. Good. The word good has been used to describe so many different things. According to Logos Bible Software, good means morally excellent. That time in my life swas great. A time to focus on God and not the world of high school. His word, and not the word of the world. Godly influence, not worldly influence. But I'm not sure if I could say it was morally excellent. Before I went to college, I had the opportunity to speak in front of my student ministry. I had already done this before, but this one was different. This was the last time I would speak before I graduated high school. I started speaking, quoted scripture, and let God say what He wanted to say. He had urged me to talk about the need to listen to His voice and His voice alone. The importance of this can't be downplayed. Ultimately, you will either listen to His voice or your time in ministry will be short lived. Let us fast forward, eighteen years, to today.

Student ministry can be a tremendous undertaking. It can cause you to question your motives and cause you to even question if it is really what you are supposed to be doing at all. That is where this simple teaching that I brought in high school pays off. See, the younger me knew; even before all of the full-time jobs were here, even before my wife was in the picture, and even before my kids came, I was going to need to listen to His voice. It is moments like this as a student pastor that make me have pride in my students.

When you see your students, step up and lead, and know that they need to follow the voice of the All Mighty, the voice of Yahweh, the voice of the one who breathed life into being, that makes it all worth it. Now that I think about it, the word good does not even begin to measure how God feels about His children who worship Him and heed the instructions from His voice. He is passionately seeking to meet us where we are, and where our students are. The only thing we must do is ask, seek, and knock, open the door, and walk into a relationship with Him.

That is what I knew as a student, and that is what I wanted to share with students, wherever God decided to put me. So many good things I had planned to do, with so many good results. This is why we need to talk about the word good, and why it can be bad. Good, good, good, good, good. How many times have you said that in your ministry? "How was youth tonight?" "Good." "You took thirty kids to youth camp?" "Yeah, it was good." Do not get me wrong, I am not against youth camps. I enjoy taking students to them and have been a part of that for over fifteen years. Taking any number of students to youth camp is a good thing. They learn Godly principles and get to have a week away from their world. But let me ask you this question. Why do we continue to measure things differently than God does? Why do we think everything we do is morally excellent?

The only time we see morally excellent is when God created everything. Seven days equals seven examples of moral excellence. How can we begin to compare the things we try to make good with the things that God made morally excellent? It is impossible. Knowing that the goodness of God is immeasurable, we can't even begin to compare what we know as good to Him.

Over the years, I have compiled a list of things that we measure, too much, by the term good:

- Attendance.

- How good was worship?

- How good was my message?

- How well do my students know the Word?

- Am I recruiting the right student ministry leaders?

- How big is the budget?

These are just a few.

I know it is hard not to look at student ministries through these lenses, but we need to evaluate the worth of good and if it is a word we should judge with . Know that I am not against these things. They are a vital piece of your student ministry, and all have a part to play, but we need to be careful of how we view them. If we are not careful, we will become a slave to good. Good will then be how we define everything around us, even if it is not "good." Let us start with attendance.

Attendance:

Picture this; You have prepared all week. You have worship all picked out, the game is ready, and you have your slides ready to go (if you use slides). You open the doors, and the students start rolling in, high fiving you as they enter. You spend time together with them and then the countdown starts. Five minutes go by on the countdown, and you watch it go to zero. Worship starts, and you pour into it and get the beat going. Once it is over, you come up on stage and pray. "Amen." The lights come on, you look up, and there are only seven students.

We, as student pastors, commonly ask, "where is everybody?" I have the answer for you. They are right in front of you. There are factors that go into the attendance of your student ministry, and I know that if students were not there, then you would not be the student pastor, but one of the biggest mistakes we make as student pastors is focusing way too much on the ones who aren't there. We must stop redirecting our focus on the ones who are not there and start living life with the ones that are. I know that this is a hard pill to swallow, but the ones who are there, are the ones that God brought to that service. Let me give you an example. Our average attendance right now is thirty students. When there are no sports, it is over forty. I am not perfect here folks. I often ask the same question, "where is everybody?" The reality is that we are focused so hard on people coming in the door, we sometimes forget that God has a plan, and it is perfect.

If His plan of salvation is perfect, then His plan, for even seven students, is far more perfect than any activity, event, or service flow we could ever create. Let me explain it in a unique way. People used to say the phrase, "Heed" my warning. This word, in the sense of giving careful attention ("take heed," "give heed," etc.), represents several Heb and Gr words; chief among them שָׁמַר, Shamar, "to watch". I want to focus on the phrase, "to watch."

We are entrusted to take care, and "to watch" the students that show up on a weekly basis. They are the ones who are there, and we do not want to lose focus on what brought them and what God has planned for them. It would be foolish to do so. My point is you cannot measure your student ministry by the number of people that are there. What you can measure is spiritual growth. How are those "seven" doing in their walk with God? What spiritual goals do they have? What have you encouraged them with? Are you praying for them?

When you take interest in the lives of your students, they will open up to you in a way that you never thought.

You become a journal of sorts. Knowing some of the most inner kept secrets that they need to surrender to God. By living life with your students, it opens the door for spiritual growth for them and for you. Then, your students will start to draw closer to God, and allow Him to change their hearts. It is only a matter of time before others see what is going on and will show up due to their own curiosity. It isn't about the attendance, it's about what you do with the ones who show up. How are you being Jesus to them? Don't judge attendance by the word good.

How Good Was Worship?

Worship…. I used to think that worship was just songs that we sang on Sunday and Wednesday, and that it was a genre of music. I honestly believed that outside of Sunday and Wednesday, Christian music was to make you feel better and to give you inspiration for the rest of the week. That is so far from the truth. The Christianese answer for, "What is worship," is, A great song to God, with loud guitars or drums. Or it could even be a light intimate song with just piano, giving praise to God. While there is not anything wrong with those terms, that is NOT the definition of what Worship is.Worship is honor, reverence, homage, in thought, feeling, or act and respect to God. Furthermore, worship is laying aside oneself and all else to recognize God. Worship is the statement that only God deserves all praise, all glory, and honor. Now that you know this, we can understand that Worship is not just simply a song we sing on Sunday's or Wednesday's, but a lifestyle. 1 Corinthians 10:31 says, "So, whether you eat or drink, or whatever you do, do all to the glory of God".

Everything we do should be a form of worship to God

and there are all diverse types of worship. Having student led praise and worship is great, but that is only one type of worship that God's word talks about. If the definition of worship is to give honor to God, we should be doing so in every area of our life. Your students will determine how to lead a life of worship based on your example.

I know that we want things to go perfect, and that when we make mistakes it can sometimes mess with our flow, but it does not mess with God's flow. Remember, we talked about God's plan being perfect. The Spirit knows what He is doing. Just because it did not go the way you wanted it to go, does not mean it is wrong or bad. I am not saying that we should not prepare, or that we should not practice. Those are perfectly fine, and you should. God did not say that once you receive His son to be lazy. But we need to see the bigger picture when it comes to your students, and worship.

Having something to offer, by this I mean, giving them a place and time for them to show this form of worship is a big step towards them living a lifestyle of worship. We have something that we do every week called, "God and I time." Once small groups are over, we have the students split off on their own. We turn the main lights off, and we play worship music in the background. They then get to spend the next five to seven minutes in uninterrupted prayer. This is part of our worship. As leaders, we try to show them that worship is more than just music, and prayer is huge. Talking to God about your day honors Him. So, do not worry about how your "worship" is. It is not the method you use, but your willingness to worship God that matters. Do not ever measure how good your student ministry is by how the music sounded, because it is not about how you heard it, but how it sounded to God.

Was My Message Good?

So, now we have the students, and we've had "worship," and we have played a game to break the ice. Now, it is time for you to speak. This can be a huge obstacle for us as Pastors and Leaders. We can base the night on what we have spoken. We might even ask those around us what they thought about the service. Don't do it.

My wife and I had gone to a conference in Ohio, for all the new church plants of that particular network. The speaker said something that I will remember forever. He said, "Your job, is to preach the Gospel of Jesus Christ." "Without fear. Without doubt. Without pride." "Don't ever ask, did you like my message?" "Because if they say yes, you'll get prideful, and if they say no, you'll want to quit so do yourselves a favor and don't ask!"

Early in student ministry, I gave a message at a conference. It was not a big conference, two or three groups. I poured over the scriptures and studied for weeks before I gave the message. Now, I cannot recall what God had laid for me to speak, but I was prepared…. Or so I thought. My wife and I drove separately, because she was going to oversee the preparations at the building for the conference, and I was going to stay at home and prepare before the event.Eventually, I made it to the conference and was getting set up for the message. The doors opened and we were ready to receive students. We prayed, had worship songs, and we were getting ready for the message. As I was getting ready to walk up to the podium, I realized that I had left my printed message at home. I was freaking out on the inside. I even remember asking myself, "God, what am I going to do now?" He replied with a simple answer. "Isn't my word enough?"

Ouch. Where was my faith? We should always be asking ourselves that question when we are preparing our messages. Where is our faith? I can honestly tell you that, that night, my faith was not in His word, but in a printed page that I had spent weeks pouring into. That night, God showed me that it was not about what I had prepared, but what He had prepared hearts to hear.

Instead of talking about what I had spent weeks planning for, I simply brought the gospel message and asked if anyone wanted to have a personal relationship with Jesus. A handful of students had their lives changed that night, all because God took control, and His plan was implemented. Wow. What an example of trusting the process. See, God was not concerned about what I had done. He was concerned about the souls that were in that room. We must trust God's plan and follow through when He reveals it to us. So how do you measure greatness in a message? How do you know if what you said hit home with your students? Discernment. You have to ask, is this God centered, or me centered? If you take yourself out of the message, does it still point to God? Remember, we need to have less of us and more of Him. When you do that, you can say that the message was a success.

How Good Do My Students Know The Word?

Okay. This one needs no introduction as it is the one that we constantly struggle with. When we sit back and look at how well our students know the word, we will more than likely start asking questions. One of the most frequent questions that I have asked is, "Why don't they do what they've learned," or "why do they keep doing this, when I've shown them what God's word says"?

These questions are normally asked out of frustration, not toward the student but their actions. When students do not do what they know the Bible says, it is only logical for you to be frustrated and to examine yourself. Examine if the problem is you, or if they even care, or maybe you don't care enough. STOP! Asking questions and being frustrated is okay, but do not let those consume you to bitterness. One thing we need to realize is that these students are still "under development" of sorts. For this, we need to know a few things about the human body.

The U.S. National Library of Medicine states that "the development and maturation of the prefrontal cortex occurs primarily during adolescence and is fully accomplished at the age of 25 years. The development of the prefrontal cortex is especially important for complex behavioral performance, as this region of the brain helps accomplish executive brain functions."

What does this mean? In simple terms, they are not ripe yet. Their ability to make complex, right, decisions are not what they will be until their early to mid-twenties. So, when you see a student being defiant or disobedient to you or a parent, remember that they are not there yet. I am not saying that they have an out, that could not be further from the truth. They must learn, sometimes through tough love, that there are consequences for their actions. The consequences for not learning the word, however, could be even more dire. Especially for others around them.

Understand, that God said, 22 But be doers of the word, and not hearers only, deceiving yourselves. These students need to be doers of the word, and they will get there. They will know more about God's word and His love, but that must be developed. Do not think for a minute that they will get this in a day. Students are all different and take various amounts of time to figure things out. Look at the disciples. The disciples did not even know exactly what they were doing when they first started following Jesus. They even fought about who they thought was the best out of all of them. But they learned.

There are things to watch out for while you lead students into the season of understanding. First, realize that you are both human. If you make a mistake, own it. Don't play the blame game, because it shows students, they do not have to take responsibility for their actions. I know that it is hard to do sometimes, but the best thing you can do is show them that you are human. Show them you make mistakes and that you correct them. Second, there will be students who never get it. You cannot make anyone grow deeper in their walk with God. That is a personal decision, a heart issue, and NOT your fault. That leads me to number three. Keep the deep connections at a minimum. I stated earlier that our job is to preach the Gospel of Jesus Christ. While we need to strive to help these students know the Bible as much as possible, we need to make sure that we keep extremely strict boundaries when it comes to relationships with them. You are where you are to lead ALL of them, not just specific ones.

Your students will learn, through your example, how deep to be in the word. Remember, these are teenagers with short attention spans and can forget what you've said as soon as you're done. Use your example and lead them to dive into God's word and remember that you cannot judge how "good" your student ministry is by how much they retain or how they choose to walk out their faith. That is a personal decision, and a heart issue on them that you cannot control.

Am I Recruiting The Right People?

How many times have we said this, "We can't find the right people for our students!" We sit there, and we promote the student ministry to people in a new members class, or we talk to people about it on Sundays and a lot of the time, all we hear are excuses that sound like, "Well that's just not my ten," or "I served there for a long time, but I want a break." Now, I am not saying that people do not have legitimate reasons for not wanting to serve in student ministry, but even when they are willing, we can be part of the problem, when it comes to recruiting. That is right, we can be part of the problem. Let me ask a question. Be honest. Are you recruiting people who you know have a willing heart that want to serve, or are you trying to recruit the ones who only bring people in? Both have their place, both do wonders for the kingdom of God, but which are you right now? What season are you in? Let us take our student ministry at my church as an example. We currently have six adults serving our students right now. Two of them brought kids in, two of them were willing to serve, but now are in a season where they bring kids in, and the other two said no but then God changed their heart.

Some of these adults asked if they were able to serve, others asked if they could serve, by my wife and I, and some said no until they listened to God. All of them were recruited. All of them were in different seasons. All of them bring different ideas into one culture. This leads to a very important point. Before you start recruiting, you must look at the current culture of your student ministry and then have a game plan about what you want the culture to look like. Once you establish that then you will be able to start recruiting. This is not a book about how to create your culture. I want to get that out of the way now. There are plenty of books out there about what culture is, and gives ideas on how to create cultures. But you cannot write a book about how to change your own culture, because everyone's culture is different, and God has a different plan for each person.

That is why each student ministry has various kinds of youth counselors, or youth teams. That will change too as God moves you from one church to the other, and when He moves your team members from your ministry, or team, to another. So, what should the criteria be? Who should I look for? The Bible points out some great tools for recruiting student leaders, counselors, or any volunteer in general. The first one is being blameless. Psalm 119:1 says, "Those whose way is blameless- who walk in the Lord's instruction- are truly happy!" Have you ever had a volunteer show up for their week to serve and they are the biggest drag? Like, do they just suck the life out of everyone else who is serving? They are constantly in an endless cycle of unhappiness? We will never be genuinely happy unless we are walking in the instruction of God. I am not saying these people cannot serve, but it is quite possible that there is sin in their life that they are unwilling to part with, and because of that they are reaping the consequences.

The second thing is, find those who are willing to change. You cannot serve well if you are unwilling to change. The story of Moses is relevant about having to change. When he was in the wilderness, before Israel's liberation, he was comfortable. He had a life and we just doing his thing. But, when he had his up-close encounter with God, God asked him to change. He even gave God every excuse to stay where he was at (Exodus 3:11). But we know how this story ends. When he stepped out of his comfort zone, he led a whole people out of bondage, slavery, and poverty to the promised land. Looking back on the years I've been in ministry, I can't help but wonder what it would have been like if I would have been willing to change sooner. Early on, I thought that only my ideas were good because I was the student pastor. I was given responsibility so if anything went wrong with someone else's idea, I would be the one that answers for it. Man did I have the wrong attitude. While it's true that I was responsible, I also limited how valuable I was as a team member. Think about it this way. In baseball, there is a position called a utility player. That means that they can play multiple positions.

It means that they are flexible and willing to step out of their comfort zone for the benefit of the team. What would happen if they stuck with their original position? They are limiting the value that they bring to the team. We have got to get into a place where we are challenged. It's too easy to get into a routine and be comfortable, which limits our value to the team. So, challenge your team. Get them out of their comfort zone. Don't help them limit the value that they bring to your team. Remember, you can only have so many first basemen. This brings me to the third point, which is, being able to lead students toward the vision God gave you. This last one is particularly important because it requires sacrifice and being willing to be sold out to the students. While it is great to have a student team that can interact well with your students, if they are unable to lead them toward the vision of the team, then they are probably not a good fit. If you currently have adults in your student team that are in this category, you may need to speak with them about changing into supportive roles and not spiritual leadership roles. If you do this, make sure it is in love, and make sure that you do it in a way that leaves answers, not questions.

The last thing is looking for someone who will be sold out. These are often hard to find as people can have versions of themselves they want you to see. I have, sadly, experienced this before. You get someone who sees the vision, knows God intimately, and everybody loves them. Only to find that they don't follow through, get angry, and have a hard time accepting criticism well. Ministry is a lifestyle, not a hobby. So when looking for your team, make sure that you explain the importance of being sold out, and if that isn't something they can do, it is totally fine, but maybe your team isn't the right fit for them.
While these are simply a few of many things you can do, they are good foundations to build your leaders on. Look for people who can:

- Be blameless

- Be willing to change

- Uphold the vision of the church, and student team

- Be sold out

Remember, you cannot judge how "good" your student ministry is based on how many adults you have. The character and fulfillment of these traits will be how to measure if they are the right fit or not.

How Big Is My Budget?

Money is the root of all evil right? Wrong! What a way to take 1 Timothy 6:10 out of context. Nowhere, in God's word, does it say that money is evil. Inanimate objects cannot be evil. The way we use them can be though, and that is why it is important to not let budgets go to your head. There are churches that have big budgets, and small budgets. Churches with accounts for each "department," and others have one account and earmark funds for each "ministry". My point is that budgets come in all shapes and sizes, depending on the church and where it is located. I could give you all the data and statistics that your little heart desires, but in the end, it will not give you what you are looking for. If you are a new church, and you need the numbers, I suggest looking at this article by, The Pacific Northwest Conference of The United Methodist Church: https://www.pnwumc.org/news/how-churches-spend-their-money/.

So, your question is, how can I reach these students with this budget? Maybe your question is, how do I use the budget I have wisely? Well, all I can say on this one is, be obedient to the Lord. That may sound like a dodge, but it is not. I could tell you to invest it all in things for the students to do, or activities. Or I could tell you to spend as little as possible to ensure that you have money for emergencies. I say all of that to say this. YOU must define the boundaries and principles for your students. YOU must have those conversations with your team and your pastor. Never be afraid to talk about money! That's right. It is not taboo or a derogatory term, it is a real conversation that must take place. Your pastor needs to know where you are, and you need to know where your pastor is. What is the number one problem in ALL churches? Communication. So, communicate with your pastor about where you are with your student ministry and have the conversation about what you want to spend. Do not judge your student ministry by how much, or how little, money you can spend. In the end, whatever your budget is, it can still be a tool to lead students to Christ, and that is the goal. So, what have we learned in this first section? You cannot judge a student ministry by the word good. When you do, you set yourself up for failure by having unrealistic expectations. When this happens, you WILL get mad. You WILL want to quit. You WILL be bitter. So, do not let good be your guide. Let God lead you to your goals and your expectations. If you are seeking Him, your wants will align with what He wants.

Before we move on to the bad, take a minute and reflect on these things.

Can you change your perspective of "good"? What impact will that have on your students?

The Bad

Okay. There are several things in student ministry that we could consider to be bad. Whether it's bad decisions on our part, or maybe a student decided to do something completely wrong on your watch, there can be many things that come up that are considered bad. Just to give you guys an inside track to a bad decision that I made; I decided it would be fun to have a dress as your favorite celebrity night. Needless to say, I ended up sending a couple students home to change. We aren't perfect, but we need to be careful of the decisions that we make. In this section, we will talk about three aspects of bad.

- How bad things happen

- How to overcome them when they happen

- How to prevent them from even being an idea in the first place.

First, I want to say that there are, at times, circumstances that are beyond our control, and we can't do anything about it. Second, I want to make it clear that everything we talk about will be scripture based, and not just thought for thought. There is enough of that happening already in the world today, and I want you to think about what God's word says and not what people think.

So, let's begin with the first one....

How Do Bad Things Happen?

How do bad things happen in student ministry? Was it me? Was it a part of my team? Was it another student? Did I not prepare enough? There can be many factors that go into bad things happening in ministry, but I want to focus on one specific type of bad thing. Pride. Pride WILL be at the epicenter of ALL bad decisions that are made. I don't mean to sound like a jerk on this, but it is true. There was a time when I had decided that we would have service on Sunday nights instead of Wednesday. To me, it was no big deal. Didn't have to worry about sports or any other school functions. I didn't pray about it, didn't ask my team about it, I didn't even really talk to my wife about it, and we are supposed to be a team. I just decided. Six months in, we had stymied growth, a burnt out student ministry team, and I had one very frustrated wife. I also did not have a great relationship with the Lord during that time. Overwhelmed and obsessed with numbers and growth, I did not see the bad in what I was doing. I was prideful, and because of it, the students suffered.

Now, I am not saying that trying new things is bad. Trying something new shakes things up and gets us out of our comfort zone. The only problem is when we make these types of decisions on our own without prayer. A simple google search says that pride is taking pleasure in one's own achievements. In Proverbs chapter 16, God gave us warning about pride and that it comes before we fall. When we reshaped the student ministry, it fell.

I fell in my leadership, I fell in my relationship with God, and I fell in my relationship with my family. I had to get my faith jump started again, and it was all due to pride. When it comes to bad things in ministry, you have to guard your heart from pride. We talked about pride a little bit in the "the good" section. You can be proud of what your students have done for God, and you can be proud to serve God in your capacity, but you should not be proud of what YOU accomplish, because we can't accomplish anything alone. God is the one who has allowed you to do what you do, so don't get too proud! Pride is hungry. If you let it creep into your life of ministry, it will devour everything. Once it devours your calling, it will then devour your family, and none of it is okay.

How To Overcome Bad Things:

Have you ever heard someone say, "bad things happen, and there's nothing you can do about it"? I have, and it just kills me to hear it. Really!? You can't do anything? To some extent there is truth to that because you can't be everywhere at once. But I believe with my whole heart that with God, you CAN do something. There is this thing that God has given us access to called wisdom. Wisdom? What is that? I'm glad you asked. Wisdom is practicing what you know, plain and simple. I remember when I was a kid, my parents would always tell me not to play in the street, or to look both ways before crossing the road. There is wisdom in that. They knew what the consequences could be if they let me do those things without instruction.

Let me just say for the record that, the attitude they had was not faithless, or out of fear. There is a difference between being faithless and having wisdom. Faith is when I didn't look both ways, my parents believed that God would protect me. Wisdom is knowing the dangers and acting on that. I think this is a good analogy to use in this section. All of you are or will be parents at some point, and there are those of you that will be as a parent to some of your students. When approached with an unpleasant situation, you have two options. The first option is to brush it off, like it is nothing, and the second is to share wisdom. You CAN do something about it. You must look for the warning signs. Warning signs come in all shapes and sizes, but you often know when one of your students will be involved in something bad when their heart isn't right. Look at their attitude. It could be their body language. Maybe they are the super hyped one that seems to be quiet and to themselves. They could even stop coming to church all together.

A wise son makes a glad father,

but a foolish son is a sorrow to his mother.

Proverbs 10:1

I have seen several students in ministry decide that they want to follow God, but they do not wish to get rid of the world. You can tell them repeatedly to let go and give their whole heart to God, but in the end, it is completely up to them. To work towards overcoming the bad in student ministry, you must see the warning signs in your students. Yes, this takes time. No, you will not be able to catch every bad thing that happens.

Here is the bottom line. Wisdom is a part of growing in your walk with God. You can't figure out how to overcome bad things on your own, and you certainly can't gain wisdom without making a few mistakes along the way.

The important thing is to include the Almighty in ALL you do. He is the ultimate source of wisdom.

Reflection:

How are you doing, at this very moment, when it comes to wisdom?

Are you learning from your mistakes, and applying what you learn?

Do you struggle with prideful thinking? What steps are you prepared to take to overcome it?

How To Prevent The Bad:

Now we've come to the section I've been looking forward to. This is the section where your problems are all going to be solved. Just kidding. Do not let the title of this section deceive you. There is no way you can prevent every bad thing from happening. You can't control anyone's actions but your own, nor should you want to. We talked in the previous section about knowing the signs or looking for changes in your students to prevent bad from happening. The difference between looking for signs and things happening are these:

- You are not omnipresent. (You cannot be everywhere at once)

- You are not omniscient. (You don't know everything)

- You are not all powerful. (You can't force anyone to do something they don't want to do)

In other words, you are not God. The best way you can prevent things from happening on your watch is to do the best you can to follow God and to do what God calls you to do. I have learned that the best way to do these things is to not set students up for failure, but to allow space for God to move. I can't guarantee you that there won't be students that get sick, or kids won't be defiant. What I can tell you is that creating a safe space for your students to be in, that allows the spirit to move in their lives, is going to be the biggest factor in preventing bad things.

Now, you might be asking the question, "well how does that help me? Why didn't you just tell me that you don't have the answer? The issue with giving you an answer, on how to prevent bad things from happening, is that it's a loaded question. We often think to ourselves, "well what if I tried this, or what if we just brought more student ministry leaders in. Maybe that will fix the problem". When we try to fix things outside of the realm of God, we set ourselves up for failure, and the more we try the more we fail. The more we fail, doing things alone, the more we want to quit. I remember a season where my wife and I had a way, or order, that we did things. We had it down to a science. I mean, no one did it, right? We had worship then prayer, and then we had a game that went with the message. After the message, we would pray and hang out and then go home. I mean it seemed like perfection. Then something bad happened that messed with "our" flow. After service that night, I talked with my pastor and he gave me something that I will never forget. He said, "It's not about what you do, but it's about what you allow God to do". What a concept right?! I know that it sounds super common sense, but how many times do we overlook common sense to try and fix things ourselves?

It's not about fixing things when it comes to bad, it's about creating an atmosphere that God can move in and then letting Him move. So, when it comes to preventing bad things, are you creating the atmosphere that allows God to move? Or are you just there to preach and go home? Because, whichever one you are will determine the amount of bad you have in your student ministry. I have been on both sides of this spectrum, and I can tell you that it is so much easier to let God be in control over you trying to make things happen.

Reflection:

Take a few minutes and write down some ways that you can improve on creating an environment that allows God to move.

The Awesome

I have titled this chapter "The Awesome", because student ministry can be just that. Awesome. There are things that happen on a weekly basis that will make you cry, excited, and appreciative of what God has you doing. The awesome can range from an activity that your students were a part of, or it could be a breakthrough. Before we start diving into some of these things, let's define awesome.

The definition of awesome is causing or inducing awe, inspiring an overwhelming feeling of reverence, admiration, or fear. When God shows up, anything is possible. That is why I have said a few times to create a space for God to move. He is the one who causes the "awe" moments in ministry. Here are just a few things that I have seen God do.

- Students accepting Christ

- Breakthrough in their lives

- Restoration in relationships

- Forgiveness

All of these are perfectly good examples of what God will do when you give Him the space to do it. I cannot say it enough that it has nothing to do with you, and everything to do with God. Let me ask you this question. Why are you in student ministry? Are you here to lead? Or are you here to be a babysitter? What is the difference? When you are babysitting, you are only there to do a job and go home. When you lead, you invest. You sacrifice. You own it. I don't know about you but I most certainly want to lead. Let's face it. Students want attention. They crave it, and they want it from whoever will give it to them and if they can't get it from their student pastor, they will get it from somewhere else, most likely the world. If you aren't ready to lead, and I don't mean this in a hateful way, then you need to step aside

because we have work to do and we want them to have some awesome for their lives. We want them to experience all the awesome they can now, before they become adults. Let's talk about a few things that we can do to lead students to the awesome.

- Partnering with parents (Deutoronomy 5:6)

- Connecting with students (Ephesians 4:11-16)

- Being present (Show up) (1 John 4:19

- Having the hard conversations (2 Timothy 3:16)

These are just a few things that I do on a regular basis with students. Let's start with connecting with parents.

Partnering With Parents:

This is at the forefront of what we do. You remember the question I asked earlier? Are you here to lead or to babysit? Sadly, I feel like there are more student pastors who are in the latter. They view student ministry as a job and not a lifestyle. Remember babysitter versus leader? That is what we are talking about here. When you view ministry as a job, you don't connect with students on a deeper level and you definitely don't speak to their parents, unless they are in trouble. It's not all their fault either. Don't misunderstand me, there are a lot of good student pastors that are babysitters, but that should not be our goal. If you want to reach students, you need to partner with their parents. You need to create a relationship that roots into the family. So how do we connect with parents? This is actually easier than you think. Let's think about your students for a minute. Do you have them sign in? If not, you should change that immediately. This is vital for two reasons. Number one, security. You can assure parents that their child was there at the designated times of your student service. Number two, you now have parent's contact information. You have opened the door to connect with the family via text, phone call, or even email. We do this every week and it has paid dividends.

Alright, you've collected contact information but what else could you do to connect with parents? I personally greet them. If they just dropped off their child I try to catch them at the end of service when they are picking them up. Making the effort to do this tells them that they are valuable and you are interested in the success of their student. One of the things we have done is creating a facebook group with all of the parents in it for information regarding the students. This was hard at first, but once it was done, we were able to establish communication with eighty to ninety percent of our parents on a weekly basis. While it isn't one hundred percent it is still more than it used to be.

You might even ask, Why is it important to partner with parents? Why can't we just partner directly with the students? The answer is not as simple as you would like. It can range from students lying, or having trust issues. It could be that dad isn't around and you are the only male role model in that student's life. Partnering with parents will help you fill in the gaps surrounding students, and it will get you in the door with others in the family. The deeper you dig the more trust you will have. The more trust you have the more your students will listen to the words you say, and look at the things you do. I can tell you from experience that partnering with parents has not only grown our attendance in our group, but it has grown faith in the family. If you haven't partnered with parents yet, I encourage you to do so. It is a win-win every time.

Connecting With Students:

So you want to connect with your students huh? That is the real reason you've bought or downloaded this book right? What is the secret to connecting with teenagers? Just like the answer to partnering with parents, the answer to this is simple. BE REAL! Yes, I yelled right now. This is something that takes years for some student pastors to figure out. Students don't want a buddy and they don't want a teacher, they want someone who is real. If all you ever do is preach to them, they WILL tune you out. Now, will God's word return void if you only preach at them?

No, it never returns void, but you might have fewer students on your service night.

Ministry is never about preaching a sermon, and it sure isn't about numbers. Ministry is relational. Why do you think churches hire staff? It isn't because the church requires worship, kids, students, or associate pastor. It is because ministry is relational and a lead pastor cannot do it alone. They cannot build worship team relationships and student relationships at the same time. That is why we have different ministry positions. This is why it is important to invest in your students. It is your job to get to know them on a personal level. Connecting is having hard conversations and fun conversations. It is cheering them on during a sporting event and crying with them when they lose a family member or a friend. It is being what your students need you to be when they need it. We recently had a student of ours lose their aunt. While it may not seem like a big deal at the time, my wife and I attended the funeral. We helped run a live stream of the service so other family members could be present virtually. Both the student and the parent were very appreciative, not only for us being there but being willing to serve them in that particular way. We were what they needed when they needed it.

Building relationships, and connecting with your students, will bring you another step closer to having a successful student ministry. Remember when we were talking about the good and how we shouldn't measure the success of a student ministry by attendance? That is very true, but you can measure the success of a student ministry by how relational you are. So here is the big question. Are you able to connect with students? If you aren't very good at connecting with students do NOT panic. You wouldn't be the only one and you most certainly aren't the first one to have this problem. If you are new to student ministry it's likely outside of your comfort zone right now and that is okay. Remember, you aren't there for you anyway. The best way to connect with your students is to be real. Do NOT hide who you are or what God has called you to do.

Being Present:

Being present is a culmination of partnering with parents and connecting with students. It is also more than just physically being in a room. It is showing life wherever you are. It's being caught up in the moment in whatever you are doing. Here is an example. Let's use football. When you see teams playing the great sport of football, you only see the part of the team that is on the playing field? You don't see the offense out on the field when the team is on defense. They are present but they aren't showing life. The same could be said of a basketball team and their benched players. They are present but they aren't really showing life until they get into the game.

Well… you need to get into the game. So how do you get in the game? It is easier than you think. Unlike sports, all you have to do is ask God, "the coach" to put you in. That's it! It's that easy. It may be uncomfortable and you may not even know what's going on, or what you are doing, but you will be present and your students will know it. Growth comes from being present. If you want to build closer relationships, both with parents and students, you WILL need to become present. It doesn't matter if you want to or not. It is a MUST. Otherwise your relationships with parents and with students will grow stagnant and you will cause more harm than good.

Reflection:

How are you partnering with parents and students? What changes do you need to make in order to be ever present in the lives of your students?

Write these down and take some time in prayer.

Ask God for guidance in these areas.

Summary And Prayer

No matter where you are or what you do, you will always have a role to play in the lives of your students. From the time they start high school to well into their adult lives, you will make an impact. The question you need to ask yourself is, what will my impact be? Follow up with this question. How could you do better? Don't be afraid to ask questions, get uncomfortable, and MAKE MISTAKES! The only way to grow and learn is by making mistakes. Ask any leader in the ministry and they will tell you that they have learned a lot of what they know through making mistakes. The bottom line is this. No matter what you do, do it for the Lord. Do it for the kingdom of God. Create spaces for Him to move in and then let Him. Don't put a limit on what God can do and watch what He does with your ministry. I'm excited for you, I'm praying for you, and I'm rooting for you. Let's pray.

"God, create in me a burning desire to be present with my students, connect with their parents, and step out of my comfort zone.

Teach me not to judge my students by good and show me the path to awesome for the ministry that I'm in.

God, you lead, and I WILL follow.

Amen".

Notes

References in order of appearance;

Grenz, S. J., & Smith, J. T. (2003). In Pocket Dictionary of Ethics (p. 47). Downers Grove, IL: InterVarsity Press.

Orr, J. (1915). Heed. In J. Orr, J. L. Nuelsen, E. Y. Mullins, & M. O. Evans (Eds.), The International Standard Bible Encyclopaedia (Vols. 1–5, p. 1367). The Howard-Severance Company.

Crannell, P. W. (1915). Worship. In J. Orr, J. L. Nuelsen, E. Y. Mullins, & M. O. Evans (Eds.), The International Standard Bible Encyclopaedia (Vols. 1–5, p. 3110). The Howard-Severance Company.

Sharma, S., Arain, M., Mathur, P., Rais, A., Nel, W., Sandhu, R., Haque, M., & Johal, L. (2013). Maturation of the Adolescent Brain. Neuropsychiatric Disease and Treatment, 9(9), 449–461. https://doi.org/10.2147/ndt.s39776

The Pacific Northwest Conference of The United Methodist Church: https://www.pnwumc.org/news/how-churches-spend-their-money/

The Holy Bible: English Standard Version (Wheaton, IL: Crossway Bibles, 2016), Pr 10:1.

www.dictionary.com, Awesome:Feb. 2022

9 789356 673755